Cleaner Tomorrow: Strategies for Preventing Pollution Today

In a world where pollution and environmental degradation are becoming increasingly pressing issues, it is more important than ever to focus on prevention. Cleaner Tomorrow is a book that provides strategies and techniques for preventing pollution, protecting our planet, and creating a better future for generations to come.

With contributions from leading experts in the field, this book offers a comprehensive guide to pollution prevention, covering a wide range of topics including waste reduction, resource conservation, and sustainable manufacturing practices. It explores how individuals, businesses, and governments can work together to reduce pollution, and outlines the economic, social, and environmental benefits of doing so.

Whether you are an environmental professional, a concerned citizen, or simply interested in learning more about pollution prevention, Cleaner Tomorrow is a valuable resource for anyone who wants to make a positive impact on the world around us. Join us as we explore the strategies and techniques that will help us build a cleaner, healthier, and more sustainable tomorrow.

Chapter 1: The Importance of Pollution Prevention

Definition Of Pollution Prevention

Pollution prevention refers to the practices and strategies aimed at reducing or eliminating the amount of waste and pollution generated by human activities. It involves a proactive approach to address the root causes of pollution and to reduce or eliminate the need for pollution control measures. The goal of pollution prevention is to minimize the environmental impact of human activities while promoting sustainable economic development.

Why Pollution Prevention Is Important

Pollution prevention is important for several reasons:

Protecting human health: Pollution can have adverse effects on human health, ranging from minor irritation to life-threatening illnesses. By preventing pollution, we can reduce the risk of these negative health impacts.

Protecting the environment: Pollution can have a significant impact on the environment, harming wildlife and ecosystems. By preventing pollution, we can help protect the natural world and the resources it provides.

Economic benefits: Pollution prevention can result in cost savings for businesses and communities. By reducing waste and increasing efficiency, pollution prevention can lead to lower operating costs and greater economic stability.

Compliance with regulations: Many jurisdictions have regulations in place to limit pollution. By preventing pollution, businesses and individuals can avoid fines and other penalties for noncompliance.

Overall, pollution prevention is essential for creating a healthy and sustainable future for ourselves and future generations.

The Benefits Of Pollution Prevention

Pollution prevention offers numerous benefits, including:

Protecting human health: Pollution prevention reduces the exposure of harmful pollutants to humans, which can result in a range of health problems, from respiratory issues to cancer.

Protecting the environment: Pollution prevention helps protect ecosystems and biodiversity, reducing the harm caused to wildlife and natural habitats.

Cost savings: By preventing pollution, businesses can reduce the costs associated with pollution control, remediation, and compliance.

Increased efficiency: Pollution prevention often involves process improvements that can increase the efficiency of operations, reduce waste, and conserve resources.

Enhanced reputation: By adopting pollution prevention practices, companies can demonstrate their commitment to environmental stewardship and social responsibility, which can enhance their reputation with stakeholders.

Compliance: Pollution prevention can help businesses meet regulatory requirements and avoid fines and penalties for noncompliance.

Innovation: Pollution prevention can spur innovation in product design, process engineering, and technology development, leading to new products and services that meet customer needs while reducing environmental impacts.

The Costs Of Pollution

The costs of pollution can be significant and far-reaching. Pollution can lead to negative impacts on human health, the environment, and the economy. Some of the costs of pollution include:

Health costs: Exposure to pollution can cause a wide range of health problems, including respiratory illnesses, cancer, and heart disease. The costs of treating these illnesses can be substantial, and they can also result in lost productivity and income.

Environmental costs: Pollution can damage ecosystems, harm wildlife, and reduce the quality of air, water, and soil. This can have far-reaching effects on agriculture, fishing, and other industries that depend on healthy ecosystems.

Economic costs: Pollution can result in lost income and productivity, as well as increased healthcare costs and environmental remediation expenses. It can also lead to decreased property values and reduced tourism revenues.

Overall, the costs of pollution can be significant and long-lasting, and they can have far-reaching impacts on individuals, communities, and the planet as a whole. This is why pollution prevention is so important.

Chapter 2: Understanding the Causes of Pollution

Overview Of The Different Types Of Pollution

Pollution can take many forms, and can impact the environment and human health in a variety of ways. Some of the most common types of pollution include:

Air pollution: This refers to the release of harmful substances into the air, such as carbon dioxide, sulfur dioxide, and particulate matter. Air pollution can cause respiratory problems, contribute to climate change, and damage ecosystems.

Water pollution: This occurs when harmful substances are released into bodies of water, such as rivers, lakes, and oceans. Water pollution can harm aquatic life, make water unsafe for human consumption, and damage ecosystems.

Soil pollution: This refers to the contamination of soil by harmful substances, such as heavy metals, pesticides, and other chemicals. Soil pollution can make land unsuitable for agriculture or other uses, and can also harm human health.

Noise pollution: This refers to excessive or unwanted sound that can disrupt human activities and cause health problems, such as hearing loss, sleep disturbance, and stress.

Light pollution: This occurs when artificial light sources, such as streetlights and buildings, produce excessive or unnecessary light that can disrupt natural patterns and cause harm to wildlife and ecosystems.

Plastic pollution: This refers to the accumulation of plastic waste in the environment, which can harm wildlife, pollute waterways, and contribute to climate change.

Understanding The Causes Of Pollution

Understanding the causes of pollution is an essential step in preventing it. Pollution can come from a wide range of sources, including human activities, natural events, and the interactions between the two. Here are some common causes of pollution:

Industrial processes: Factories and other industrial facilities can release harmful chemicals and pollutants into the air, water, and soil.

Transportation: Cars, trucks, and other vehicles produce air pollution through their exhaust fumes. They can also contribute to water pollution through oil and other leaks.

Agriculture: Fertilizers, pesticides, and animal waste from farming operations can cause water pollution and soil contamination.

Energy production: Burning fossil fuels such as coal and oil to generate electricity can release harmful pollutants into the air.

Waste disposal: Improperly disposing of waste can lead to water and soil pollution.

Natural causes: Pollution can also come from natural events such as volcanic eruptions and wildfires.

By understanding the different causes of pollution, we can take steps to prevent it and protect our environment.

Pollution Prevention Versus Pollution Control

Pollution prevention involves identifying and eliminating the source of pollution before it is released into the environment. In contrast, pollution control involves managing or treating pollution that has already been released into the environment. While pollution control measures can help to reduce the impact of pollution, pollution prevention is considered more effective and sustainable in the long term. By preventing pollution at the source, we can reduce the amount of pollution that needs to be treated or managed and reduce the overall impact on the environment and public health.

Chapter 3: Pollution Prevention Strategies

Overview Of Pollution Prevention Strategies

Here's an overview of some of the pollution prevention strategies that could be discussed in the book:

Source reduction: This involves reducing the amount of pollution generated at the source, for example, by using less toxic chemicals or by optimizing processes to reduce waste generation.

Green chemistry: This is the design of chemical products and processes that reduce or eliminate the use or generation of hazardous substances.

Energy efficiency: This involves reducing the energy required for production processes, for example, by using energy-efficient technologies or by optimizing processes to reduce energy waste.

Waste reduction: This involves reducing the amount of waste generated by a process, for example, by recycling or by using raw materials more efficiently.

Product design: This involves designing products that are environmentally friendly and that can be easily recycled or reused.

Education and awareness: This involves educating the public and stakeholders about pollution prevention and its importance.

Government policies and regulations: This involves setting policies and regulations that encourage pollution prevention, for example, by providing incentives for companies that adopt pollution prevention strategies.

Life-cycle assessment: This involves assessing the environmental impact of a product or process throughout its life cycle, from raw material extraction to disposal.

Environmental management systems: This involves implementing a management system to systematically identify, evaluate, and control environmental impacts.

Pollution prevention audits: This involves conducting an audit of a facility or process to identify opportunities for pollution prevention.

These strategies could be discussed in more detail in the book, along with case studies and examples of successful implementation.

Source Reduction

Source reduction is a pollution prevention strategy that aims to reduce the amount of waste or pollution created at the source before it becomes a problem. This approach involves changing production processes, materials, or products to minimize waste or pollution. It can involve using more efficient manufacturing techniques, reducing the use of hazardous materials, or designing products that generate less waste. The goal of source reduction is to minimize the need for waste management and pollution control measures, and to create more sustainable and efficient production processes. Source reduction can also lead to cost savings for businesses, as they use less raw materials and generate less waste.

Recycling And Reuse

Recycling and reuse are two effective pollution prevention strategies. Recycling is the process of converting waste materials into new products to prevent the accumulation of waste in landfills or incinerators. The materials that can be recycled include paper, plastic, glass, aluminum, and steel. Reuse is the process of using a product again, usually after it has been repaired or refurbished. Examples of reusable products include water bottles, cloth bags, and rechargeable batteries.

Both recycling and reuse can significantly reduce the amount of waste generated and the need for new resources to be extracted from the environment. They also help reduce pollution by minimizing the amount of waste that ends up in landfills or incinerators, which can emit harmful substances into the air, soil, and water. Additionally, recycling and reuse can create new jobs and economic opportunities, especially in the recycling and refurbishing industries.

Energy Efficiency

Energy efficiency is a pollution prevention strategy that aims to reduce the amount of energy used to perform a task or process. By using less energy, less pollution is created, and less greenhouse gas emissions are released into the atmosphere, helping to mitigate climate change.

Energy efficiency can be achieved through various methods, such as using energy-efficient appliances, using renewable energy sources like solar and wind power, reducing energy waste by improving insulation and weather sealing, and implementing energy-efficient lighting systems. Additionally, implementing energy management systems and adopting sustainable transportation options can also help to reduce energy use and prevent pollution.

Alternative Technologies

Alternative technologies refer to the use of innovative or unconventional approaches to mitigate pollution. These technologies are aimed at reducing the amount of pollution generated or emitted by various activities. Some examples of alternative technologies that can be used for pollution prevention include:

Renewable energy technologies: These include solar, wind, geothermal, and hydroelectric power. The use of renewable energy can reduce the amount of pollution generated by burning fossil fuels.

Clean technologies: These are technologies that produce less pollution or waste than traditional technologies. Examples include clean coal technologies, which aim to reduce the amount of pollution generated by burning coal, and fuel cells, which produce electricity without combustion.

Green chemistry: This is a set of principles and practices aimed at reducing the use and generation of hazardous substances in chemical processes.

Bioremediation: This is the use of living organisms to remove pollutants from the environment. Bioremediation can be used to clean up polluted soil and water.

Nanotechnology: This involves the manipulation of materials at the nanoscale level. Nanotechnology can be used to create new materials and devices that are more efficient and generate less pollution.

Sustainable agriculture: This involves the use of farming practices that are environmentally sustainable and reduce pollution.

Integrated waste management: This involves the use of a combination of methods to reduce, reuse, and recycle waste.

These alternative technologies are just a few examples of the many innovative approaches that can be used to prevent pollution.

Sustainable Materials Management

Sustainable materials management (SMM) is a comprehensive approach to managing materials that aims to reduce environmental impacts, conserve resources, and minimize waste. It involves the full life cycle of materials, from extraction or harvesting of raw materials through their disposal or reuse.

SMM encompasses a variety of practices, including:

Design for Environment: This involves designing products and packaging with environmental considerations in mind. For example, using recyclable materials or designing products to be more durable and repairable can reduce waste and conserve resources.

Waste Reduction: This involves reducing the amount of waste generated by individuals, businesses, and industries. This can be achieved through practices such as composting, source reduction, and product stewardship.

Recycling: This involves recovering materials that have reached the end of their useful life and transforming them into new products. Recycling reduces the need for virgin materials and conserves resources.

Energy Recovery: This involves using waste materials as a source of energy. For example, waste-to-energy facilities can generate electricity by burning municipal solid waste.

Composting: This involves decomposing organic waste into a nutrient-rich soil amendment. Composting reduces the amount of organic waste sent to landfills and can be used to support healthy soil and plant growth.

SMM promotes a circular economy, in which materials are reused and recycled as much as possible, minimizing waste and conserving resources. It can also reduce greenhouse gas emissions and support sustainable economic growth.

Chapter 4: Pollution Prevention in Practice

Examples Of Successful Pollution Prevention Strategies In Various Industries

Here are a few examples of successful pollution prevention strategies implemented in various industries:

Automotive Industry: The automotive industry has been successful in implementing pollution prevention strategies by adopting lean manufacturing processes, reducing waste, and recycling. For example, Honda has implemented a "zero-waste-to-landfill" initiative, which involves recycling and repurposing almost all of its waste.

Chemical Industry: The chemical industry has implemented pollution prevention strategies by adopting green chemistry principles, reducing waste, and designing safer chemicals. For example, DuPont implemented a pollution prevention program that resulted in a 70% reduction in waste and a 40% reduction in energy use.

Food Industry: The food industry has implemented pollution prevention strategies by reducing waste, using sustainable packaging, and implementing water conservation measures. For example, Nestle implemented a water stewardship program that resulted in a 40% reduction in water usage across its manufacturing facilities.

Electronics Industry: The electronics industry has implemented pollution prevention strategies by reducing the use of hazardous chemicals, improving energy efficiency, and recycling electronic waste. For example, Apple implemented a recycling program that recovers valuable materials from old devices and reuses them in new products.

Agriculture Industry: The agriculture industry has implemented pollution prevention strategies by reducing the use of pesticides and fertilizers, adopting conservation tillage practices, and using precision agriculture technologies. For example, the Sustainable Agriculture Network has implemented a certification program that encourages farmers to adopt sustainable practices and reduce the environmental impact of their operations.

These are just a few examples of successful pollution prevention strategies in various industries.

Case Studies Of Companies And Organizations Implementing Pollution Prevention Techniques

Here are a few examples of companies and organizations implementing pollution prevention techniques:

3M: The manufacturing company 3M implemented a pollution prevention program that resulted in a 64% reduction in hazardous waste generation, a 75% reduction in air emissions, and a 48% reduction in water use. The program included measures such as source reduction, recycling, and process improvements.

Ford Motor Company: Ford implemented a pollution prevention program that aimed to reduce the environmental impact of its manufacturing processes. The program included measures such as waste reduction, energy efficiency, and the use of sustainable materials. As a result of these efforts, Ford was able to reduce its water use by 25%, reduce its energy use by 30%, and cut its greenhouse gas emissions by 40%.

University of Wisconsin: The University of Wisconsin implemented a pollution prevention program that focused on reducing the use of hazardous chemicals on campus. The program included measures such as source reduction, chemical substitution, and employee training. As a result of these efforts, the university was able to reduce its hazardous waste generation by 44%, reduce its chemical use by 60%, and save over $500,000 in disposal costs.

Xerox: Xerox implemented a pollution prevention program that aimed to reduce the environmental impact of its manufacturing processes. The program included measures such as waste reduction, energy efficiency, and the use of sustainable materials. As a result of these efforts, Xerox was able to reduce its greenhouse gas emissions by 18%, reduce its energy use by 10%, and cut its water use by 16%.

Procter & Gamble: Procter & Gamble implemented a pollution prevention program that aimed to reduce the environmental impact of its manufacturing processes. The program included measures such as waste reduction, energy efficiency, and the use of sustainable materials. As a result of these efforts, Procter & Gamble was able to reduce its greenhouse gas emissions by 7%, reduce its energy use by 7%, and cut its water use by 4%.

Chapter 5: Government Regulations and Pollution Prevention

Overview Of Government Regulations Related To Pollution Prevention

Government regulations related to pollution prevention include laws, policies, and programs that aim to reduce or eliminate pollution at its source. These regulations may be implemented at the local, state, or federal level and can cover various aspects of pollution prevention, including air, water, and soil pollution, as well as hazardous waste management.

Some examples of government regulations related to pollution prevention include the Clean Air Act, the Clean Water Act, and the Resource Conservation and Recovery Act. These laws establish minimum standards for the release of pollutants into the environment and set requirements for the treatment and disposal of hazardous waste.

In addition to these laws, many government agencies also offer pollution prevention programs and incentives to encourage companies and organizations to reduce their environmental impact. For example, the U.S. Environmental Protection Agency (EPA) offers grants, technical assistance, and training programs to support pollution prevention efforts across various industries.

Overall, government regulations related to pollution prevention play an essential role in ensuring that companies and organizations are held accountable for their environmental impact and encouraging them to adopt more sustainable practices.

The Role Of Government In Promoting Pollution Prevention

The role of government in promoting pollution prevention is crucial. Governments have the power to regulate and enforce pollution prevention measures, as well as to provide incentives and support for industries and individuals to adopt sustainable practices. Some ways in which government can promote pollution prevention include:

Enforcing regulations: Governments can enforce regulations related to pollution prevention to ensure that industries and individuals are complying with environmental standards. This can include penalties for non-compliance and incentives for those who meet or exceed standards.

Providing incentives: Governments can provide incentives such as tax breaks, grants, and subsidies to industries and individuals who adopt sustainable practices that prevent pollution. This can encourage companies to invest in pollution prevention technologies and individuals to adopt environmentally friendly lifestyles.

Education and outreach: Governments can educate the public about the importance of pollution prevention and provide outreach programs to help people learn how to prevent pollution in their daily lives. This can include campaigns to reduce waste, increase recycling, and promote energy efficiency.

Research and development: Governments can fund research and development of new pollution prevention technologies and methods. This can help drive innovation and make it easier and more cost-effective for industries and individuals to adopt sustainable practices.

Overall, the role of government in promoting pollution prevention is essential for creating a sustainable future for all.

The Relationship Between Regulation And Innovation

Regulation can have a significant impact on innovation in pollution prevention. By setting clear standards for pollution reduction and prevention, governments can create a market demand for new and innovative pollution prevention technologies and techniques. This, in turn, can incentivize companies and researchers to invest in developing these technologies, which can lead to new discoveries and improvements in pollution prevention. On the other hand, overly burdensome or unclear regulations can stifle innovation by making it difficult for companies to invest in research and development or comply with regulations. Thus, striking a balance between effective regulation and innovation is critical in promoting pollution prevention.

Chapter 6: Pollution Prevention in the Community

The Role Of Individuals And Communities In Preventing Pollution

Individuals and communities play a critical role in preventing pollution. They can make choices in their daily lives that contribute to reducing pollution, such as reducing their use of single-use plastics, conserving energy, and using public transportation. Individuals and communities can also organize and advocate for pollution prevention measures, such as promoting the use of clean energy sources, supporting sustainable agriculture practices, and advocating for government policies that promote pollution prevention.

In addition, individuals and communities can participate in local initiatives that promote pollution prevention, such as participating in community clean-up events, supporting local businesses that prioritize sustainability, and educating others about the importance of pollution prevention.

By taking action at the individual and community level, people can make a significant contribution to preventing pollution and promoting a cleaner, healthier future for everyone.

Community-Based Pollution Prevention Initiatives

Community-based pollution prevention initiatives refer to the efforts of local groups, organizations, and individuals to prevent pollution in their own communities. These initiatives aim to raise awareness about the issue of pollution and its impacts, engage community members in taking action, and implement solutions to reduce pollution at the local level.

Examples of community-based pollution prevention initiatives include:

Adopt-a-Street programs: Community groups and organizations adopt a street or area in their neighborhood and commit to regularly cleaning up litter and other forms of pollution.

Community gardens: These initiatives involve the creation of community gardens where members of the community can grow their own produce using sustainable and organic gardening practices, reducing the need for transportation and packaging associated with commercially grown produce.

Waste reduction and recycling programs: Community groups and organizations can initiate programs to reduce waste and increase recycling, such as composting, waste reduction campaigns, and recycling education programs.

Environmental education and awareness campaigns: These initiatives aim to raise awareness about the impacts of pollution on human health and the environment, and educate individuals and communities on ways to prevent pollution.

Green infrastructure projects: These initiatives involve the installation of green infrastructure, such as green roofs, rain gardens, and permeable pavements, to reduce stormwater runoff and improve water quality.

Community-based pollution prevention initiatives can have a significant impact on reducing pollution at the local level and building more sustainable communities.

Education And Outreach Efforts

Education and outreach efforts can be an effective way to promote pollution prevention and encourage individuals and communities to take action. This can include:

Public awareness campaigns: Governments and environmental organizations can run public awareness campaigns to educate the public about the impact of pollution on the environment and human health, as well as the benefits of pollution prevention.

Environmental education: Schools and community organizations can provide education and training on pollution prevention and sustainable practices, such as recycling and energy efficiency.

Community programs: Communities can develop programs that encourage individuals and businesses to take steps to prevent pollution. For example, a city might offer free home energy audits to encourage residents to improve their energy efficiency.

Voluntary initiatives: Many businesses and organizations have implemented voluntary initiatives to reduce their environmental impact. These initiatives can include setting goals for reducing waste, energy use, or other environmental impacts, and tracking progress towards these goals.

Green certification programs: Certification programs can help consumers identify products and services that are environmentally friendly. For example, a business might be certified as a "green business" if it meets certain sustainability criteria.

Overall, education and outreach efforts can help raise awareness of the importance of pollution prevention, and encourage individuals and communities to take action to reduce their environmental impact.

Chapter 7: Emerging Technologies and Innovations in Pollution Prevention

Overview Of Emerging Technologies And Innovations In Pollution Prevention

Emerging technologies and innovations in pollution prevention are diverse and rapidly evolving. Some of the most promising developments include:

Artificial intelligence and machine learning: These technologies can help predict environmental risks and identify areas where pollution prevention efforts are most needed.

Bioremediation: This involves using living organisms to break down pollutants and contaminants, either naturally or through the use of genetically modified organisms.

Carbon capture and utilization: This technology involves capturing carbon dioxide emissions from industrial processes and using them to create products such as cement, plastics, and fuels.

Green chemistry: This is a set of principles and practices aimed at reducing or eliminating the use of hazardous substances in chemical processes.

Nanotechnology: This technology involves the manipulation of matter on a molecular or atomic scale, and has potential applications in pollution prevention through improved materials design and manufacturing processes.

Renewable energy: This includes solar, wind, hydro, and

geothermal power, which can replace fossil fuels and reduce greenhouse gas emissions.

Smart sensors and monitoring systems: These technologies can track pollution levels in real time, allowing for more targeted pollution prevention efforts.

Waste reduction and recycling: Innovative methods for reducing waste and increasing the efficiency of recycling processes are being developed, such as using robotics and automation to sort and process materials.

Overall, emerging technologies and innovations in pollution prevention hold great promise for reducing the environmental impact of human activities and promoting a more sustainable future.

The Role Of Technology In Pollution Prevention

Technology plays a crucial role in pollution prevention. It provides new ways to reduce or eliminate pollution and allows for greater efficiency and cost-effectiveness in implementing pollution prevention strategies. For example, advancements in renewable energy technologies have made it possible to reduce greenhouse gas emissions and prevent air pollution from burning fossil fuels. Similarly, advancements in wastewater treatment technology have made it possible to treat wastewater to a higher standard, reducing the impact of pollutants on local waterways.

In addition, emerging technologies such as artificial intelligence, the Internet of Things, and big data analytics offer new opportunities to monitor and manage pollution sources. These technologies can provide real-time data on pollution levels, which can be used to optimize pollution prevention strategies and quickly identify and address pollution incidents.

However, it's important to note that technology alone is not enough to prevent pollution. It must be coupled with effective policies, regulations, and individual actions to create a sustainable and pollution-free future.

Examples Of Innovative Pollution Prevention Techniques

There are many examples of innovative pollution prevention techniques being developed and implemented. Some examples include:

3D printing: 3D printing allows for precise manufacturing of products, reducing waste and material use.

Bio-based materials: Researchers are developing materials made from renewable sources, such as plant-based plastics, to reduce reliance on fossil fuels.

Smart grids: Smart grids use advanced technologies to manage energy use, reducing waste and greenhouse gas emissions.

Nanotechnology: Nanotechnology is being used to develop materials and products with improved environmental performance, such as coatings that repel pollutants.

Carbon capture and storage: Carbon capture and storage technologies capture carbon dioxide emissions from power plants and other sources and store them underground.

Green chemistry: Green chemistry involves developing chemicals and chemical processes that are safer and more environmentally friendly than traditional alternatives.

Precision agriculture: Precision agriculture uses sensors and other technologies to optimize crop yields and reduce environmental impact.

These are just a few examples of the many innovative pollution prevention techniques being developed and implemented around the world.

Chapter 8: Economic and Social Benefits of Pollution Prevention

The Economic Benefits Of Pollution Prevention

Pollution prevention can have significant economic benefits. For one, it can lead to cost savings for businesses and industries. By preventing pollution at the source, companies can reduce the amount of waste they generate, which can lower disposal costs. Pollution prevention can also reduce the need for expensive pollution control technologies, which can be costly to install and maintain.

In addition, pollution prevention can help businesses comply with environmental regulations, which can result in avoiding costly fines and legal fees. By preventing pollution, businesses can also improve their reputation and marketability, which can lead to increased sales and profits.

On a larger scale, pollution prevention can also have economic benefits for society as a whole. By preventing pollution, we can reduce the health and environmental costs associated with pollution-related illnesses and cleanup efforts. This can lead to cost savings for governments, taxpayers, and businesses, as well as improved quality of life for communities. Additionally, pollution prevention can create new jobs in fields such as environmental consulting, engineering, and research and development.

The Social Benefits Of Pollution Prevention

Pollution prevention has many social benefits, including:

Healthier communities: Pollution prevention reduces the amount of harmful pollutants that are released into the environment, which can have a positive impact on the health of nearby communities. This can reduce the incidence of respiratory problems, cancer, and other illnesses.

Improved quality of life: Clean air, water, and land are essential for a high quality of life. Pollution prevention helps to protect these resources and improve the quality of life for individuals and communities.

Environmental justice: Pollution tends to be concentrated in low-income and minority communities, leading to environmental injustice. Pollution prevention can help to address these inequities by reducing the amount of pollution in these communities.

Job creation: Pollution prevention technologies and practices can create jobs in industries such as engineering, manufacturing, and environmental consulting.

Increased productivity: Companies that implement pollution prevention strategies often experience increased efficiency and productivity, as well as cost savings.

Overall, pollution prevention is an important way to improve social well-being by protecting human health, promoting environmental justice, and creating economic opportunities.

The Role Of Pollution Prevention In Creating A Sustainable Future

Pollution prevention is a critical component of creating a sustainable future. The environmental, economic, and social benefits of pollution prevention are numerous and significant. By reducing pollution at the source, we can reduce the negative impact on the environment and public health, conserve natural resources, and save money on treatment and cleanup costs.

Additionally, pollution prevention can create new business opportunities and jobs in industries focused on developing and implementing new technologies and practices. Furthermore, it can improve the quality of life in communities by reducing exposure to pollutants and increasing the availability of clean air, water, and soil.

Overall, pollution prevention is essential for achieving sustainability, as it helps to balance economic growth with environmental protection and social responsibility. By incorporating pollution prevention strategies into our daily lives and supporting initiatives that promote pollution prevention, we can work towards a cleaner, healthier, and more sustainable future for ourselves and future generations.

Chapter 9: Challenges and Opportunities in Pollution Prevention

Current Challenges To Implementing Pollution Prevention Techniques

Some current challenges to implementing pollution prevention techniques include:

Lack of awareness: Many people and businesses are not aware of the impact of pollution and the benefits of pollution prevention. Education and outreach efforts can help address this challenge.

Cost: Implementing pollution prevention techniques can require upfront investments, which can be a barrier for businesses and individuals. However, the long-term benefits of pollution prevention can outweigh the initial costs.

Resistance to change: Some individuals and businesses may be resistant to changing their current practices, even if it means reducing pollution. Addressing this challenge may require incentives, such as tax breaks or regulatory requirements.

Lack of regulation: In some areas, there may be little or no regulation related to pollution prevention, which can make it difficult to enforce sustainable practices.

Technological limitations: Some pollution prevention techniques require advanced technology, which may not be widely available or affordable. Continued research and development can help overcome this challenge.

Global cooperation: Pollution is a global problem, and addressing it will require international cooperation and coordination. Achieving this level of cooperation can be challenging due to political, economic, and cultural differences.

Opportunities For Advancing Pollution Prevention Efforts

There are several opportunities for advancing pollution prevention efforts, including:

Collaborative partnerships: Building strong partnerships between government, industry, and communities can facilitate the development and implementation of effective pollution prevention strategies.

Innovation: Continuing to invest in research and development of innovative technologies and practices can help to identify new pollution prevention techniques and improve existing ones.

Education and outreach: Raising public awareness about the benefits of pollution prevention and providing information on how individuals and businesses can reduce their environmental impact can help to promote widespread adoption of pollution prevention practices.

Policy and regulation: Establishing and enforcing regulations and policies that encourage pollution prevention can incentivize businesses to adopt these practices.

Corporate responsibility: Encouraging businesses to adopt corporate social responsibility practices that include pollution prevention can help to reduce their environmental impact and contribute to a more sustainable future.

Consumer demand: Increasing demand for sustainable products and services can drive businesses to adopt pollution prevention practices to meet consumer expectations.

By leveraging these opportunities, it is possible to accelerate progress towards a more sustainable and pollution-free future.

Future Directions For Pollution Prevention

As pollution continues to pose a significant threat to the health of our planet and its inhabitants, there are several directions that pollution prevention efforts could take in the future. Some of these include:

Advancements in technology: With the rapid pace of technological development, there are bound to be new innovations in pollution prevention. One area where we are likely to see advancements is in renewable energy, which could help reduce reliance on fossil fuels and lower greenhouse gas emissions.

Strengthening regulations: While regulations have been effective in reducing pollution in the past, there is always room for improvement. Governments around the world could take steps to strengthen existing regulations or introduce new ones to address emerging environmental challenges.

Collaboration: Addressing complex environmental issues like pollution requires collaboration between governments, businesses, and individuals. By working together, we can develop more effective strategies and create a more sustainable future.

Education and awareness: Educating the public about the impact of pollution and the importance of prevention is crucial to building a sustainable future. Through education and awareness campaigns, we can inspire individuals and communities to take action to reduce their environmental footprint.

Global action: Pollution is a global issue that requires a coordinated global response. International organizations like the United Nations and the World Health Organization can play a key role in promoting pollution prevention efforts on a global scale.

Chapter 10: Moving Forward with Pollution Prevention

Call To Action For Individuals, Businesses, And Policymakers To Prioritize Pollution Prevention

Pollution prevention is an essential step towards building a sustainable future for our planet. As individuals, businesses, and policymakers, we all have a role to play in reducing pollution and protecting our environment.

We must prioritize pollution prevention and focus on implementing sustainable practices across all industries. This includes reducing waste and emissions, promoting energy efficiency, and developing innovative solutions to prevent pollution.

It is also essential that we continue to educate ourselves and others on the importance of pollution prevention and the benefits it provides to both the environment and our communities.

As a society, we have the power to make a significant impact on the health of our planet. Let's work together to prioritize pollution prevention and create a cleaner, healthier future for generations to come.

Steps Individuals And Organizations Can Take To Prevent Pollution

There are several steps that individuals and organizations can take to prevent pollution. Here are some examples:

Reduce, reuse, and recycle: By reducing the amount of waste produced, reusing products whenever possible, and recycling materials, individuals and organizations can significantly reduce the amount of pollution they create.

Conserve energy: Energy conservation can help reduce pollution by decreasing the amount of fossil fuels that are burned to generate electricity.

Use eco-friendly products: Choose environmentally-friendly products made from sustainable materials and avoid those that contain harmful chemicals.

Properly dispose of hazardous waste: Hazardous waste should be disposed of properly to prevent it from polluting the environment.

Use public transportation, walk, or bike: Transportation is a major source of pollution, so reducing the use of cars and using public transportation, walking, or biking can significantly reduce pollution.

Support policies and legislation that promote pollution prevention: Individuals and organizations can advocate for policies and legislation that support pollution prevention efforts.

Educate others: Education and awareness-raising can help individuals and organizations understand the importance of pollution prevention and take action to prevent it.

By taking these steps, individuals and organizations can help prevent pollution and promote a healthier, more sustainable future.

Conclusion And Final Thoughts On The Importance Of Pollution Prevention

Pollution prevention is critical for the health and sustainability of our planet. The impacts of pollution can be devastating to both the environment and human health, making it essential that we take steps to reduce our impact. This book, "Cleaner Tomorrow: Strategies for Preventing Pollution Today", highlights the importance of pollution prevention and provides an overview of the different types of pollution and strategies for preventing them.

Through the case studies and examples presented, readers can see the positive impacts that pollution prevention can have on both the environment and the economy. While there are challenges to implementing pollution prevention techniques, there are also many opportunities for advancing these efforts through technological innovation, government policies, and community-based initiatives.

It is crucial that individuals, businesses, and policymakers take action to prioritize pollution prevention and take steps to reduce their impact on the environment. By doing so, we can create a cleaner, healthier, and more sustainable future for ourselves and future generations.